Did T. REX Have Feathers?

This edition published in 2021 by Arcturus Publishing Limited
26/27 Bickels Yard, 151–153 Bermondsey Street,
London SE1 3HA

Illustrator: Luke Séguin-Magee
Author: Ben Hubbard
Editors: William Potter and Violet Peto
Designer: Steve Flight

CH007048NT
Supplier: 10, Date 0621, Print run 11569

Printed in the UK

MIX
Paper from
responsible sources
FSC® C018072

CONTENTS

WHEN DID DINOSAURS LIVE?

Dinosaurs were a group of reptilian creatures that ruled the planet for over 160 million years, a time called the Mesozoic Era, made up of three shorter periods: the Triassic, Jurassic, and Cretaceous.

TRIASSIC PERIOD
(251 to 199.6 mya*)

The first dinosaurs appeared around 228 million years ago. At that time, Earth was made up of one joined-up supercontinent called Pangaea. By 216 million years ago, early dinosaurs had spread across the globe.

JURASSIC PERIOD
(199.6 to 145.5 mya*)

At the beginning of the Jurassic period, Pangaea split into two continents. As smaller landmasses broke away, new species of dinosaurs evolved within them, and the great dinosaur giants first appeared.

CRETACEOUS PERIOD
(145.5 to 65.5 mya*)

The land split into smaller continents and temperatures on Earth soared. Plant and animal life flourished, and many new dinosaur species evolved, some of them growing to extraordinarily large sizes.

* mya = million years ago

DINOSAUR DISCOVERIES

WHAT WERE THE DINOSAURS?

The dinosaurs were a group of land-dwelling reptiles that first appeared on Earth around 230 million years ago. There were hundreds of species of dinosaurs; some were gentle plant-eaters, while others were ferocious killers. After dominating the globe for 160 million years, the dinosaurs mysteriously died out around 65 million years ago.

DID YOU KNOW?

Tyrannosaurus rex (ty-RAN-oh-SORE-us REX), Triceratops (try-SEH-ra-tops), and Edmontosaurus (ed-MON-toe-sore-us) lived in North America during the Late Cretaceous period (76-65 million years ago).

WHAT DID DINOSAURS LOOK LIKE?

Dinosaurs came in a staggering selection of different shapes, sizes, and shades. Some dinosaurs were taller than a three-floor building and weighed more than 12 elephants. Other dinosaurs were no bigger than a chicken. Certain dinosaurs had scaly, camouflaged skin and lumbered around slowly on four legs. Others were covered with bright feathers and ran around nimbly on two legs.

WHAT DOES "DINOSAUR" MEAN?

When the first dinosaur remains were unearthed in the 19th century, scientists were not sure what they had discovered. They named the owners of the huge fossilized bones "dinosaurs," which means "fearfully great lizards."

DID YOU KNOW?

Dinosaurs were different from other reptiles because their legs were positioned directly beneath them, rather than splayed out to the sides.

HOW DO WE KNOW ABOUT THE DINOSAURS?

We have learned everything we know about dinosaurs from the remains they left behind. These include fossilized bones and skeletons, footprints preserved in rock, and fossilized dinosaur dung. By studying these remains, scientists are able to establish what the dinosaurs looked like, how they moved, and what they ate.

WHAT'S INSIDE DINOSAUR DUNG?

Preserved dinosaur dung is called coprolite, and it reveals what dinosaurs were eating millions of years ago. Scientists have discovered pieces of bone, parts of plants, and fish scales inside dinosaur coprolite.

HOW DID DINOSAURS LEAVE FOOTPRINTS?

Many dinosaurs left their footprints in soft, swampy ground that later dried in the sun and became hard. Over time, these footprints were buried under sand, mud, and water and became fossilized. This made the footprints as solid as stone. Dinosaur footprints tell us how much a dinosaur weighed, how it walked, and whether it was moving in a herd.

DID YOU KNOW?

Fossilization occurs when an animal or plant becomes preserved over time.

WHAT DO YOU CALL A DINOSAUR EXPERT?

Scientists that study dinosaur fossils are called paleontologists. They are not the same as archaeologists, who study past human life and activities.

WHAT IS A FOSSIL?

A fossil is the remains of an animal or plant that has been buried underground and preserved in rock. Fossils are mostly made up of the harder parts of an animal, such as its teeth or bones, rather than its softer body parts. Imprints such as footprints and feathers can also be fossilized. A fossil can be as small as a tooth or claw, or as large as a complete dinosaur skeleton.

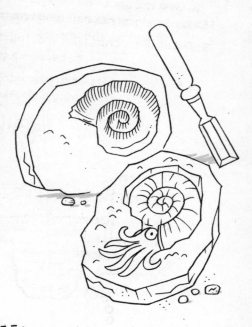

WHAT IS AN AMMONITE?

An ammonite is a common fossil of a shelled sea creature from the time of the dinosaurs.

HOW IS A FOSSIL MADE?

1. A fossil is formed when the remains of a creature are covered over by sand, mud, or sediment. Over time, the soft body parts rot away, leaving behind the hard bones and teeth.

2. Over millions of years, layers of earth cover the remains. Fluids containing minerals seep into gaps in the bone and teeth.

3. The minerals crystallize and, together with the bone, harden to become a fossil.

4. Millions of years later, paleontologists discover the fossil during a dinosaur dig.

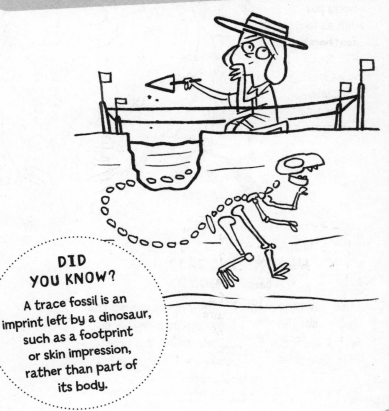

DID YOU KNOW?

A trace fossil is an imprint left by a dinosaur, such as a footprint or skin impression, rather than part of its body.

WHO DISCOVERED THE DINOSAURS?

The first dinosaur remains were discovered by accident in the English countryside. In 1822, Mary Ann Mantell and her husband, Dr. Gideon Mantell, found what looked like giant lizard teeth and several large bones buried in the ground. The couple continued to dig for more bones, until a fuller picture of the creature emerged.

WHICH DINOSAUR HAD BEEN FOUND?

After much research, Dr. Mantell concluded that the teeth and bones belonged to a reptile that resembled a giant iguana, He called this creature Iguanodon (ig-WAH-noh-don), which means "iguana tooth."

WHAT DID IGUANODON LOOK LIKE?

To begin with, Mantell thought that Iguanodon walked on four legs, had a spike on its nose, and dragged its tail along the ground. His theory changed after the remains of 40 Iguanodons were discovered in a Belgian mine in 1878. The skeletons were pieced together to show that Iguanodon walked on two legs, had a spike on its thumb instead of its nose, and kept its tail off the ground.

DID YOU KNOW?
Iguanodon grew up to 10 m (32 ft) long and 5,000 kg (11,000 lb) in weight.

WERE ALL DINOSAURS RELATED?

There were hundreds of different species of dinosaur, but all belonged to an ancient family called archosaurs, or "ruling reptiles." Modern crocodiles and birds also belong to this family—so did a range of strange and startling creatures that lived alongside the dinosaurs during the Mesozoic Era.

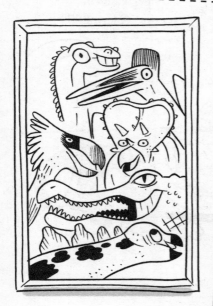

WHAT IS AN ARCHOSAUR?

Archosaurs are a group of creatures that share some common physical features. These can best be seen in their skulls. All archosaurs have an opening in front of their eye sockets called the antorbital fenestra, which helps them breathe. Another opening near the back of the lower jaw contains muscles for a strong bite.

WHAT DID THE ANCESTORS OF DINOSAURS LOOK LIKE?

Euparkeria (yoo-PAR-kare-ee-uh) was one of the oldest-known archosaurs and an ancestor to the dinosaurs that followed. With scaly skin, a back covered in small, bumpy plates, and sharp, pointed teeth, Euparkeria walked on two legs and preyed upon small vertebrates.

DID YOU KNOW?

Euparkeria was an archosaur that lived in South Africa during the Early Triassic period (252-247 million years ago). It grew up to 70 cm (28 in) in length, 20 cm (8 in) tall, and 7-14 kg (15-31 lb) in weight.

WHAT WERE THE FIRST DINOSAURS?

The first true dinosaurs were small meat-eaters, such as Eoraptor, that appeared in South America during the Late Triassic period. Measuring up to 2 m (6.5 ft) tall, these predators had curved finger claws, hollow limb bones for speed, and skulls that absorbed shock when biting prey. They would evolve into the large, killer dinosaurs.

DID YOU KNOW?

The meat-eating dinosaurs were "bipedal," which means they walked on two legs.

DID EORAPTOR EAT MEAT?

Around 1 m (3 ft) in length, Eoraptor (EE-oh-rap-tor) is often regarded as one of the earliest dinosaurs. Standing on two legs with two small arms, Eoraptor resembled the large predators that followed. However, there was one big difference. Eoraptor's jaw contained a combination of knifelike and leaflike teeth, meaning it must have fed on both meat and plants to survive.

DID PLATEOSAURUS WALK ON TWO FEET OR FOUR?

Plateosaurus (PLAT-ee-oh-SORE-us) was a Late Triassic period plant-eater that lived across the plains of Europe. A large number of fossilized skeletons, both adults and juveniles, have been found in modern-day Germany. Plateosaurus was a link between the two-footed meat-eating dinosaurs and the large four-footed plant-eaters. This is because Plateosaurus normally walked on four feet, but it could also stand on two feet to pick the leaves from treetops. It was the first dinosaur to be able to eat high vegetation; before it, plant-eaters were stumpy with a short neck, so they foraged nearer ground level.

DID YOU KNOW?

Plateosaurus was 7 m (22 ft) long and weighed up to 4,000 kg (8,800 lb).

WHAT WERE THE MAIN TYPES OF DINOSAURS?

Dinosaurs are divided into two main groups and are classified according to the shape of their hip bones. The two types of dinosaurs are saurischians, which means "lizard-hipped," and ornithischians, which means "bird-hipped."

WHO WERE THE SAURISCHIANS?

Saurischian dinosaurs were meat-eating and plant-eating dinosaurs that had hip bones like those of modern lizards. This means they had two lower hip bones that pointed in opposite directions. T. rex was one of the most famous saurischians.

ORNITHISCHIAN

SAURISCHIAN

DID YOU KNOW?

Although ornithischian means "bird-hipped," modern birds actually evolved from saurischian dinosaurs.

WHO WERE THE ORNITHISCHIANS?

The ornithischians were plant-eating dinosaurs, and they had hip bones shaped like those of modern birds. Ornithischian hip bones lay together and faced backward, which gave them more stability when they were walking.

Some of the ornithischian dinosaurs were four-footed giants, such as the massive Brachiosaurus (BRAK-ee-oh-SORE-us). Other ornithischians, such as Heterodontosaurus (HET-er-oh-DONT-oh-sore-us), walked on two legs, and some, such as Iguanodon, could walk on both.

DID YOU KNOW?

Heterodontosaurus means "different-toothed lizard," and although it looked like a meat-eater, it actually ate plants.

WHEN DID THE DINOSAURS LIVE?

The dinosaurs lived, thrived, and died out during the Mesozoic Era, which lasted for 180 million years. The Mesozoic Era was broken into three shorter ages: the Triassic, Jurassic, and Cretaceous periods. The dinosaurs appeared around 230 million years ago during the Late Triassic period. By the end of the Cretaceous period, they were extinct.

DID YOU KNOW?

During the Triassic period, the Earth was spinning faster than it does today. Back then, one day was only 23 hours long.

WHAT WAS **THE TRIASSIC PERIOD LIKE?**

During the Triassic period, the Earth's continents were joined together in a large landmass called Pangaea. Pangaea was a vast place, with a hot, dry desert in the middle. Near the coastal regions, new animal life and the first forests appeared.

WHAT WAS **THE JURASSIC PERIOD LIKE?**

During the Jurassic period, Pangaea divided into two huge continents. New oceans and waterways began to form, and there was more oxygen in the atmosphere. Many forms of plant and animal life evolved at this time.

 TODAY

TRIASSIC

JURASSIC

CRETACEOUS

WHAT WAS **THE CRETACEOUS PERIOD LIKE?**

During the Cretaceous period, the continents split into smaller continents, similar to those we have today. Life thrived at this time. Flowering plants appeared, and dinosaurs evolved into over 250 different types. The climate was mild during the Cretaceous period, and the North and South Poles did not have permanent ice sheets.

WHAT WIPED OUT THE DINOSAURS?

Around 65 million years ago, a gigantic, catastrophic event killed off over 75 percent of all life on Earth, including the dinosaurs. Most scientists agree that this mass extinction was caused by an asteroid. They believe a 24-km (15-mile) wide asteroid hurtled toward the Earth at twice the speed of a bullet and struck an area near modern-day Mexico.

HOW DID THE DINOSAURS DIE OUT?

The impact of the asteroid hitting the Earth was like a million atom bombs exploding at once. First, there was a massive shock wave, followed by tsunamis, fires, and hot dust, which filled the sky. As the dust cooled, it left a thick black cloud that lasted for months and blocked the Sun. Without sunlight, plant and animal life died out.

DID ALL THE DINOSAURS DIE AT ONCE?

It would have taken many months for the dinosaurs to become extinct. The first to go were the large plant-eaters, which depended on huge amounts of plant life to survive. This left the meat-eaters with no food, so they would have died out shortly after, followed by the smaller dinosaurs. Some forms of animal life survived the mass extinction, including crocodiles.

WHAT OTHER CREATURES SURVIVED THE DINOSAUR EXTINCTION?

Creatures that survived largely unchanged include frogs, snakes, turtles, sharks, and many insects and arachnids (such as spiders and scorpions). Dragonflies survived the dinosaur extinction and have existed on Earth for over 300 million years.

DID YOU KNOW?

The asteroid that caused the dinosaur extinction left a massive crater 180 km (112 miles) wide.

ARE ANY DINOSAURS ALIVE TODAY?

No dinosaur survived the mass extinction. But some creatures that are directly descended from the dinosaurs share the planet with us today. We know these creatures as birds. The descendants of other creatures that lived alongside the dinosaurs still live on Earth, too.

HOW ARE BIRDS DESCENDED FROM DINOSAURS?

Over time, the dinosaurs developed the characteristics that they passed on to modern birds. These include feathers, beaks, clawed fingers, and bony tails. One dinosaur that closely resembled a bird was Caudipteryx (caw-DIP-ter-iks). Caudipteryx was the size of a turkey and covered in feathers, but it had the teeth and bones of a dinosaur.

DINOSAUR PLANET

WHAT WAS THE DINOSAUR WORLD LIKE?

The dinosaur world was one of continual change. Over millions of years, hundreds of different dinosaur species appeared and died out again, as the Earth underwent its own vast changes. During the time of the dinosaurs, every imaginable environment came and went: deserts, swamps, wetlands, forests, tundra, and open plains.

WHICH DINOSAURS PLUNDERED THE PLAINS?

The plains of the Late Cretaceous period were dominated by herds of plant-eating dinosaurs. These included the ceratopsians: horned and frilled dinosaurs such as Centrosaurus (SEN-troh-sore-us), Styracosaurus (sty-RAK-oh-sore-us), and Chasmosaurus (KAZ-moh-sore-us). The ceratopsians were hunted by predators such as Albertosaurus (al-BERT-oh-sore-us).

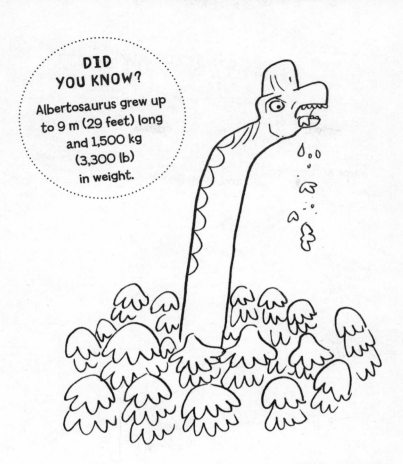

WHO RULED THE FORESTS?

The forests of the Cretaceous period were home to some of the most ferocious dinosaurs, such as Tyrannosaurus rex and Troodon (TROH-oh-don). They hunted plant-eaters such as Kritosaurus (KRIT-oh-sore-us), a duck-billed dinosaur that fed on low-lying shrubs. The forests were also the domain of the large plant-eaters, such as Diplodocus (DIP-loh-dock-us) and Stegosaurus (STEG-oh-sore-us).

WHICH REPTILES RULED THE SKIES?

While dinosaurs dominated the land during the Mesozoic Era, a different group of reptiles ruled the air. These flying predators were called pterosaurs, or "winged reptiles," and they were the terror of the skies. However, pterosaurs were not only confined to the air—they hunted land and sea creatures as well.

DID RHAMPHORHYNCHUS HAVE FEATHERED WINGS?

Like all pterosaurs, Rhamphorhynchus (RAM-for-ink-us) did not have feathered wings for flying. Instead, it had leathery wings covered with skin, like those of a bat. Attached to the wings were clawed fingers used to catch and grip prey. Light, hollow bones helped Rhamphorhynchus stay airborne.

WAS QUETZALCOATLUS THE LARGEST FLIER?

With a wingspan of 12 m (39 ft), Quetzalcoatlus (KWETS-ul-koh-AT-lus) is believed to be one of the largest fliers of all time. No one is sure whether Quetzalcoatlus hunted mostly at sea or on land, but studies have shown it could have flown for long distances looking for food. Its top speed in the air is believed to be 128 km/h (80 mph).

DID YOU KNOW?

Pterodactylus (TEH-roh-DACK-till-us) was the first-ever pterosaur to be discovered.

WHICH REPTILES CONTROLLED THE SEAS?

While dinosaurs were the reptiles that lived on land, and pterosaurs were the reptiles that ruled the air, a different group of giant reptiles dominated the seas. These massive marine reptiles were equipped with sleek, streamlined bodies to help them swim easily through the water and seek out their prey. Dakosaurus (DACK-oh-sore-us) was a marine predator around the size of a large crocodile that lived during the Early Cretaceous period.

WAS KRONOSAURUS BIGGER THAN A SHARK?

Kronosaurus (KRON-o-sore-us) was one of the largest and most lethal creatures to live in the sea, and it would have dwarfed a modern-day shark. Belonging to the pliosaur group of marine reptiles, Kronosaurus could reach up to 10 m (33 ft) long and weigh around 1,000 kg (2,204 lb). It had a short neck, broad flippers, and a long jaw. It used its powerful bite to grip and then crush its prey.

WHY DID ELASMOSAURUS HAVE A LONG NECK?

Elasmosaurus (el-LAZZ-moh-SORE-us) belonged to a group of marine reptiles known as plesiosaurs, which often had long necks, similar to sauropod dinosaurs on land. It is thought that Elasmosaurus used its long neck to grab hard-to-reach prey and flick them quickly into its mouth.

DID YOU KNOW?

Elasmosaurus grew up to 14 m (46 ft) in length and 2,000 kg (4,400 lb) in weight.

WERE ALL DINOSAURS MEAT-EATERS?

Dinosaurs enjoyed three different types of diet. Herbivores ate plants, carnivores ate meat, and omnivores ate everything. Theropods, such as the Tarbosaurus (TAR-boh-sore-us) in this picture, were large flesh-eating dinosaurs. They needed to consume huge amounts of meat every day. But not all carnivores were giant-sized killers. Some survived by eating insects and lizards.

DID YOU KNOW?

Tarbosaurus grew up to 13 m (43 ft) in length and 6,350 kg (14,000 lb) in weight.

DID ALL MEAT-EATERS HAVE SHARP TEETH?

Not all two-legged dinosaurs had sharp teeth. Gallimimus (gal-ee-MY-mus) was about the size of a turkey and had a beak instead of a snout. It used this beak to eat aquatic insects and crush up seeds.

DID YOU KNOW?

Tarbosaurus used its powerful jaws and bone-crunching teeth to kill its prey.

WHAT DOES "THEROPOD" MEAN?

All of the meat-eating dinosaurs belonged to the theropod group, which means "beast-footed." Large theropods were perfectly designed killing machines with a big head, thick neck, and powerful legs. These predators would use their feet to hold down their prey and tear off chunks. Smaller theropods, such as Struthiomimus (stroo-thee-OH-meem-us), were quick and agile and used their long claws to hunt.

WHAT DID A DIPLODOCUS EAT?

A Diplodocus's diet would have included conifer leaves, ginkos, ferns, and mosses.

WERE MANY OF THE DINOSAURS PLANT-EATERS?

Most of the dinosaurs were herbivores, which means they ate plants. Some herbivores, such as Triceratops, were low to the ground and had horns and beaks. Others, such as Hadrosaurus (HAD-roh sore-us), had less protection but developed special teeth to chew their food. The herbivores known as sauropods grew to sizes never seen before or after on Earth.

WHAT WERE HERBIVORE TEETH LIKE?

Herbivore dinosaurs had different teeth from the carnivores. Instead of sharp, serrated teeth, they had peg-, leaf-, and diamond-shaped teeth to tackle the particular plants they ate. The large sauropods had teeth for stripping the leaves from trees but none for grinding them. This is because they needed to eat almost constantly to feed their giant bodies; they did not have time to chew!

DID YOU KNOW?

Triceratops had a beak to tear up hardy plants and tough teeth to slice through them.

HOW DID DINOSAURS REPRODUCE?

Dinosaurs gave birth by laying eggs, as reptiles and birds do today. Some dinosaurs, such as Oviraptor (OH-vee-rap-tor), sat on their eggs to warm them. Others, such as Argentinosaurus (AR-jen-tee-noh-sore-us), laid thousands of eggs in colonies and left them to hatch by themselves.

DID DINOSAURS EAT EGGS?

Meat-eaters would have found eggs and young hatchlings an easy meal. Some dinosaurs guarded their nests. Protoceratops laid their eggs in a circle of hollowed-out ground with a wall of earth to protect them. They stayed close to the nest to protect it against predators.

DID DINOSAURS SIT ON THEIR NESTS LIKE BIRDS?

Oviraptor guarded its own nest— a hollow dug in the ground. We know it sat on its eggs until they hatched.

WHAT WAS A DINOSAUR EGG LIKE?

Dinosaur eggs had a hard outer casing, like birds' eggs, and came in several shapes and sizes. Most were elongated, but the eggs of Diplodocus were the size and shape of a soccer ball. Maiasaura's (MY-ah-sore-ah's) eggs, shown here, were oval-shaped and were the size of grapefruit.

DID YOU KNOW?

Maiasaura means "good mother lizard." The preserved remains of baby Maiasaura were discovered inside its egg case.

DID DINOSAURS LIVE IN HERDS?

For many plant-eating dinosaurs, living in a herd provided safety in numbers. Giant sauropods, such as Saltasaurus (SOL-tuh-sore-us), kept their babies in the middle of the herd where they could be protected. Large adults stayed on the outside of the herd to watch out for predators.

DID DINOSAURS MIGRATE?

Large sauropods are likely to have migrated during the summer months, much like herds of zebra do today. By looking at fossils of sauropod teeth and analyzing what they ate, scientists can track the dinosaurs' movements. It is thought that they moved from the plains to upland areas in search of food each summer. Dinosaur trackways have been found all over the world, from Canada in the north to Australia in the south.

HOW DO WE KNOW DINOSAURS LIVED IN GROUPS?

The fossilized trackways of sauropod dinosaurs show that many roamed together in herds. The smaller, lighter footprints of the young sauropods confirm that they were protected in the middle of the group. Ancient fossilized footprints of 23 running sauropods were found in San Antonio, Texas, in 1940.

DID YOU KNOW?

Sauropod trackways from Texas show the giant Sauroposeidon running at around 7.2 km/hour (4.5 mph).

HOW DID DINOSAURS COMMUNICATE?

Plant-eating dinosaurs warned each other of danger by flushing their body parts with blood, flapping their feathers, or making loud noises. Some developed special ways of making themselves heard. Parasaurolophus (pa-ra-sore-OLL-off-us) used the crest on top of its head to make honking and hooting sounds. A recent theory suggested that the warning noises a Parasaurolophus made sounded like a foghorn on a boat.

HOW DID PARASAUROLOPHUS HONK?

Parasaurolophus was a hadrosaur with a long crest running over the top of its head. Inside the crest was a hollow tube that connected to Parasaurolophus's nose and mouth. Parasaurolophus was able to blow through this natural trumpet to warn others of danger and also use the sound to attract mates. Other hadrosaurs, such as the Saurolophus pair below, might have used their crests in a similar way.

WHY DID PARASAUROLOPHUS NEED A WARNING SIGNAL?

Parasaurolophus needed a good warning device as it had no claws, plates, or sharp teeth for protection.

WHAT DID DINOSAUR SKIN LOOK LIKE?

Dinosaurs may have come in a broad range of shades, from dull greens and browns to bright reds, yellows, and blues. However, for years, no one was sure what dinosaur skin was like. Then in 2002, scientists discovered the skin pigmentation of a Sinosauropteryx (sine-oh-sore-OP-ter-iks) under a microscope. It showed that Sinosauropteryx was reddish brown, covered in feathers, and had a striped tail.

WHAT SHADES WERE DINOSAURS?

The giant sauropods are thought to be drab shades, such as green and brown. The meat-eaters were probably striped and spotted like a leopard or tiger to help camouflage them when they were hunting.

HOW THICK WAS DINOSAUR SKIN?

Dinosaur skin was tough and scaly like that of modern reptiles. The skin had to be strong enough to not tear easily but flexible for freedom of movement. It also had to be waterproof to protect against the elements. Waterproof skin prevents an animal from drying out in the sun as well as keeping liquid from getting in.

DID ANY DINOSAUR SKIN SURVIVE?

Dinosaurs left their skin behind as fossilized imprints. These show us the texture of the dinosaur's skin but not its shade.

WHAT CREATURES LIVED WITH DINOSAURS?

During the Mesozoic Era, dinosaurs were the dominant land creatures. However, they shared their world with a large assortment of different species of birds, insects, reptiles, and mammals. The remains of some of these creatures have been found preserved around lakes, such as these in China:

Manchurochelys (MAN-chur-oh-kell-us), an ancient type of turtle

Confuciusornis (KON-few-shus-or-nis), an early bird

Hyphalosaurus (high-FAH-loh-sore-us), a swimming lizard

Peipiaosteus (pay-PYOW-stee-us), a fish

Liaoconodon (lee-ah-CON-oh-don), an early mammal

GIGANTIC DINOSAURS

WHO WERE THE LARGEST DINOSAURS?

The largest dinosaurs were the plant-eating sauropods. The sauropods had bulky bodies, tiny heads, tall legs, and incredibly long tails and necks. The design of a sauropod is much like that of a crane on a building site. Its bulky body kept it from toppling over.

DID THE SAUROPODS HAVE BIG BRAINS, TOO?

Although sauropods were the biggest dinosaurs, they had very small brains.

WHEN DID THE SAUROPODS LIVE?

Sauropods first appeared around 200 million years ago, during the Early Jurassic period. However, the most famous sauropods, such as Diplodocus, did not emerge until around 150 million years ago. During the Cretaceous period, the sauropods began to decline, and by the time of the dinosaur extinction, only smaller sauropods such as Nemegtosaurus (nem-egg-tow-sore-us) and Rapetosaurus (ra-PET-oh-sore-us) were left. Of course, they were only small by sauropod standards: Rapetosaurus could grow to 15 m (49 ft) in length, which is longer than a bus.

WAS BRACHIOSAURUS THE BIGGEST DINOSAUR?

When the bones of Brachiosaurus were discovered in 1903, scientists believed it to be the biggest creature that ever walked the planet. Brachiosaurus was longer than three buses and heavier than nine elephants. But despite its enormous size, Brachiosaurus was dwarfed by an even bigger dinosaur discovered in 1993: Argentinosaurus.

WHAT WAS THE BIGGEST SAUROPOD OF ALL?

As long as four buses and weighing more than 12 elephants, Argentinosaurus was the biggest sauropod of all. It lived in South America during the Late Cretaceous period.

HOW TALL WAS A BRACHIOSAURUS LEG?

Brachiosaurus was unusual for a sauropod dinosaur because its front legs were longer than its back legs. Its front legs were taller than a human and kept the head of the dinosaur raised upward. This helped the dinosaur reach the highest leaves at the tops of tall trees.

WHY DID BRACHIOSAURUS HAVE A BUMP ON ITS HEAD?

Brachiosaurus's skull was formed into a distinctive dome at its top, which is where its eyes and nostrils were placed. It is thought that the dome may have housed a special sound chamber for Brachiosaurus to call to its herd.

DID YOU KNOW?

Brachiosaurus lived in North America and Africa in the Late Jurassic period (155–140 million years ago).

49

COULD DIPLODOCUS STAND ON ITS BACK LEGS?

Diplodocus was one of the longest dinosaurs. Its enormous tail may have been used to balance its very long neck. Diplodocus may have made itself even taller by standing on its back legs to reach the highest branches. If it did so, its tail would have rested on the ground and helped prevent it from toppling over.

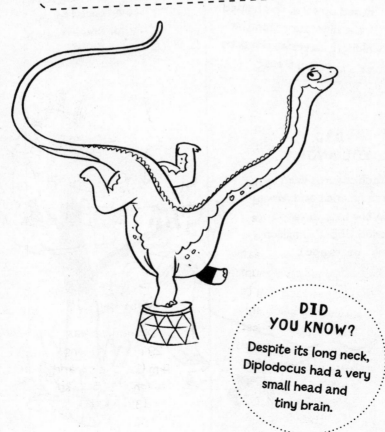

DID YOU KNOW?

Despite its long neck, Diplodocus had a very small head and tiny brain.

HOW DID DIPLODOCUS EAT?

Diplodocus had distinctive pencil-shaped teeth that were arranged like a rake at the front of its jaws. There were no back teeth to chew, so Diplodocus spent its time raking leaves off the trees and swallowing them. Although it could reach the treetops, it is thought that Diplodocus kept its head horizontal most of the time, sweeping its head backward and forward like a vacuum cleaner over the trees.

WHY DID PLANT-EATERS HAVE LONG NECKS?

The giant sauropod dinosaurs had long necks to reach the high leaves that other plant-eaters could not reach. Because they were so large, sauropods had to eat a tremendous amount of leaves each day to survive. By being able to reach the highest leaves, the sauropods were not competing with other smaller herbivores for their food.

DID YOU KNOW?

Diplodocus was 29 m (95 ft) long, 4 m (13 ft) high, and weighed 14,500 kg (32,000 lb).

HOW DID THE GIANT PLANT-EATERS GET SO BIG?

The sauropods became so big by making themselves the ultimate eating machines. They did this by developing their bodies to consume the greatest number of calories as quickly as possible. This was made possible by the blossoming of new plant and forest life that took place during the Jurassic period.

DID YOU KNOW?

Mamenchisaurus (mah-MEN-chee-sore-us) grew up to 22 m (75 ft) long, 6 m (20 ft) high, and 22,700 kg (50,000 lb) in weight.

HOW MUCH DID THE SAUROPODS EAT?

A large sauropod like Diplodocus had to eat around 520 kg (1,150 lb) of plant material every day just to survive. The biggest sauropod, Argentinosaurus, probably had to eat even more. As it grew from a 5 kg (11 lb) hatchling, Argentinosaurus gained up to 40 kg (90 lb) of weight every day. It took around 40 years for Argentinosaurus to reach its maximum weight of 75,000 kg (165,350 lb).

HOW DID THE SAUROPODS DIGEST THEIR FOOD?

Because the sauropods ate so much, they did not have time to chew their food. Instead, they swallowed it whole and left their stomach to do the rest. To help with this task, sauropods swallowed stones called gastroliths, which helped grind up their food. When a gastrolith became too smooth, the sauropod expelled it and swallowed a new one. Piles of smooth gastrolith stones have been found among dinosaur fossils in the Morrison Formation, a large series of rock layers in North America.

DID THE GIANT PLANT-EATERS HAVE ENEMIES?

For every large plant-eater that walked the Earth, there was also a large meat-eater to rival it. On the plains of South America, Argentinosaurus evolved into the biggest dinosaur the world has ever known. However, at the same time, a great meat-eater grew alongside it: Giganotosaurus. It is unlikely that a Giganotosaurus would have tried to bring down an Argentinosaurus by itself, but it probably hunted in packs to do so.

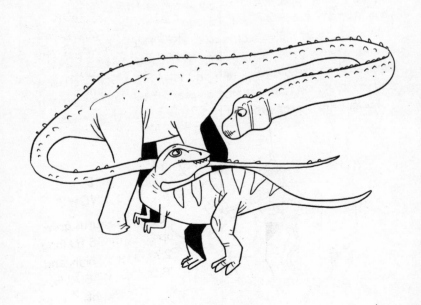

HOW BIG WAS GIGANOTOSAURUS?

Giganotosaurus (gig-an-OH-toe-sore-us) was the largest meat-eating dinosaur of South America in the Cretaceous period, and a terror to any plant-eater that crossed its path. Giganotosaurus weighed more than two elephants, was as long as two buses, and had jaws full of long, serrated teeth, ideal for slicing through bone and flesh.

WAS T. REX RELATED TO GIGANOTOSAURUS?

Giganotosaurus roamed the Earth 30 million years before T. rex existed, and the two were not directly related. Instead, Giganotosaurus was related to another huge killer called Carcharodontosaurus (kar-KAR-oh-don-toh-sore-us). However, Carcharodontosaurus lived in Africa, and there was no chance of it battling Giganotosaurus for dominance.

DID YOU KNOW?

Giganotosaurus grew up to 14 m (46 ft) long, 2.75 m (9 ft) high, and 8,000 kg (17,600 lb) in weight.

WHO WAS THE BIGGEST PLATED DINOSAUR?

Ankylosaurus was the tank of the dinosaur world. The largest member of the ankylosaur family, Ankylosaurus was armed with deadly weapons, covered in impenetrable plates, and weighed as much as a small bus. Ankylosaurus needed this level of protection; the plant-eater lived during the time of the terrifying tyrannosaurs.

WAS ANKYLOSAURUS A FAST MOVER?

Although it was well designed to defend itself, Ankylosaurus had a small brain and was not adapted for fast movement. This meant that the dinosaur had a slow, plodding walk and was unlikely to pick up any speed. However, the part of Ankylosaurus's brain that controlled smell was well developed, and it would have been able to easily detect a predator's scent.

DID YOU KNOW?

Ankylosaurus grew up to 7 m long (22 ft), 2.75 m (9 ft) tall, and 7,000 kg (15,430 lb) in weight.

WHAT WAS ANKYLOSAURUS'S TAIL CLUB MADE FROM?

The solid round club at the end of Ankylosaurus's tail was one of the most effective weapons of the Cretaceous period. Weighing as much as the dinosaur's skull, the club was made of a mix of bone, tendons, and plates, fused together into a compact mass.

The bony deposits that formed the club are called osteoderms. A blow from the tail would be enough to seriously injure or kill an attacking meat-eater.

DID YOU KNOW?

Some Ankylosauruses were very bulky and could grow to over 2 m (6.5 ft) wide.

HOW LONG WERE TRICERATOPS'S HORNS?

Triceratops, or "three-horned face," was named after its short nose horn and two long brow horns. The dinosaur's nose horn was only around 30 cm (12 in) long, but its sharp brow horns could reach 1 m (3 ft) each. These provided protection against predators such as T. rex.

DID YOU KNOW?

Triceratops could reach 9 m (30 ft) in length, 3 m (10 ft) in height, and weighed 5,500 kg (12,000 lb).

WHY DID SOME DINOSAURS HAVE FRILLS?

There were several reasons why some dinosaurs had bright neck frills. These were used to signal to other dinosaurs, attract mates, scare off predators, and possibly collect heat from the sun. Triceratops' large, bony frill also protected its neck from dinosaur bites.

DID YOU KNOW?

Triceratops lived in North America around 67-65 million years ago, during the Late Cretaceous period.

DID TRICERATOPS LIVE IN HERDS?

Experts think Triceratops lived alone or in small family groups. However, many plant-eating dinosaurs did move in herds for protection against large meat-eaters. In a herd, dinosaurs could warn each other of danger and join together against predators.

WAS T. REX THE BIGGEST TYRANNOSAUR?

The most famous, feared, and ferocious dinosaur of all time, Tyrannosaurus rex was the great heavyweight of the Cretaceous period. T. rex's terrible reputation was well founded: It was the biggest and most powerful of all of the tyrannosaur predators, and one of the most spectacular killers that has ever walked the planet.

WHAT WERE T. REX'S TEETH LIKE?

T. rex's teeth were among the largest teeth of any land creature and could easily crunch through bone.

DID T. REX HAVE A BIG BRAIN?

T. rex had one of the largest and most developed brains of the predatory dinosaurs. The part of the brain responsible for smell was particularly acute. T. rex was also armed with forward-facing eyes, which gave it binocular vision and a greater ability to sense depth. These senses combined to give T. rex a formidable advantage over its prey.

WHY WAS T. REX SO SCARY?

T. rex grew up to 12 m (39 ft) long, 4.3 m (14 ft) tall, and 7,000 kg (15,400 lb) in weight. It is the sheer size and strength of T. rex that makes it seem so terrifying to us. Its skull alone was nearly as long as a grown man, and it contained sharp, serrated teeth the size of bananas. T. rex's powerful jaws gave it a bite three times stronger than a lion's. In addition, T. rex was longer than a bus, taller than two men, and heavier than an elephant.

DID T. REX HAVE FEATHERS?

In recent times, it has been suggested that T. rex had a layer of feathers around its head, although no one can be sure.

WHY DID T. REX HAVE SUCH SMALL ARMS?

It is often asked why a predator as powerful as T. rex had such small and skinny arms. There is a simple answer: It didn't need strong arms. Instead, it used its enormous jaws and teeth to bring down prey, and then held them down with its massive clawed feet as it devoured them.

DID YOU KNOW?

The arms of a T. rex were too short to push it upright if it fell over. But, like birds today, it didn't need arms. It would have stood by pulling its legs under its body, then pushing up.

WHAT DID T. REX USE ITS ARMS FOR?

T. rex may have had small arms in comparison to the rest of its body, but they were not useless. Its arms were longer than a 5-year-old boy's. Although its arms were too short to reach its mouth, its sharp claws allowed it to grip struggling prey before taking a bite.

WHAT DID T. REX SOUND LIKE?

The terrible roar that T. rex makes in the movies is not thought to be accurate. Based on the size of its neck and its skull bones, T. rex probably made a grumbling or croaking sound, like a crocodile or a bullfrog.

COULD THE DINOSAURS RUN?

Because dinosaurs could walk, it is likely that most would have been able to run. To work out a dinosaur's rough speed, paleontologists measure the distance between fossilized dinosaur footprints and the size of the tracks. But they need to find a good set of prints to do this!

HOW FAST COULD THE MEAT-EATERS RUN?

T. rex could make short sprints at a top speed of 29 km/h (18 mph). Smaller meat-eaters were often faster. Velociraptor and Dilophosaurus could both reach speeds of about 39 km/h (24 mph).

HOW FAST COULD BRACHIOSAURUS RUN?

Sauropods such as Brachiosaurus were so large that they had to keep three feet on the ground while moving to support their weight. It was unlikely that Brachiosaurus would have been able to manage more than a lumbering 8 km/h (5 mph).

KILLER DINOSAURS

WHO WERE THE GREATEST KILLER DINOSAURS?

Enormous predatory dinosaurs were the terror of the Mesozoic Era. These fearsome killers stalked and hunted live prey, scavenged meat from dead carcasses, and even ate one another. The most famous and ferocious of the large predators included T. rex, Allosaurus (AL-oh-saw-rus), and Tarbosaurus.

DANGER

KEEP YOUR DISTANCE

DID YOU KNOW?

Tarbosaurus could grow up to 10 m (32 ft) in length, 4.3 m (14 ft) in height, and 6,350 kg (14,000 lb) in weight.

WHO WAS TARBOSAURUS?

A close relative of T. rex, Tarbosaurus was a terrifying meat-eater that stalked the plains of Mongolia during the Late Cretaceous period. Tarbosaurus's skull, however, was longer than T. rex's, and it contained over 60 teeth, each one longer than your finger. Tarbosaurus used these bone-crunching teeth to tear apart large hadrosaur dinosaurs like Saurolophus (sore-oh-LOAF-us).

WERE ALL KILLER DINOSAURS LARGE?

Not all the dinosaur predators were immense: Some were the size of a cat. Others, like Saurornithoides (sore-OR-nith-oid-eez), were slightly taller than a man, ran on two feet, and were armed with claws and sharp, serrated teeth. Although these speedy little predators tended to feed on small mammals, they were still dangerous hunters.

DID YOU KNOW?

Saurornithoides could grow to 3 m (10 ft) long and up to 30 kg (65 lb) in weight.

WHAT WERE A KILLER DINOSAUR'S WEAPONS?

Every meat-eating dinosaur had a deadly array of weapons in its arsenal to hunt down and kill its prey. These weapons included teeth, claws, and jaws, but size, speed, and strength also helped. Most importantly, the predators needed bigger brains than their prey to outsmart them.

DID YOU KNOW?

Megaraptor grew up to 8 m (29 feet) long and weighed up to 1,815 kg (4,000 lb).

WHICH KILLER HAD LETHAL CLAWS?

An unusual predator called Megaraptor (MEG-a-rap-tor) had one of the most lethal claws ever discovered on a dinosaur. Megaraptor was an 8 m (26 ft) long monster with a sickle-shaped hand claw that measured 35 cm (14 in) long. That's longer than a fork! The claw was the longest of several claws that Megaraptor used to slash open its prey.

DID YOU KNOW?

Megaraptor lived in South America during the Late Cretaceous period.

WAS DEINONYCHUS THE ULTIMATE RAPTOR?

Deinonychus (die-NON-i-kus) was one of the smartest members of the infamous "raptors", a group of midsized predators that attacked their prey with killing claws. Unlike its larger meat-eating counterparts, Deinonychus was equipped with a large brain, a body built for speed, and precision weapons for a fast and efficient kill. When Deinonychus was discovered in 1964, it showed the world that dinosaurs could be small, smart, and speedy.

HOW DID DEINONYCHUS KILL WITH ITS CLAWS?

Deinonychus was armed with claws on both of its hands and feet, but each foot also featured an extra-long "killing claw." The palms of Deinonychus's hands faced inward, which helped the predator clutch onto its prey. Once in its grip, Deinonychus would deliver a lethal blow to its victim with one of its killing toe claws.

WHO DID DEINONYCHUS HUNT?

The most common of Deinonychus's prey was the plant-eating Tenontosaurus (ten-ON-toe-sore-us). We know this because a deposit of fossils found in North America revealed several Deinonychus skeletons around those of a Tenontosaurus. This fossil find also proved that the raptor hunted in packs.

DID YOU KNOW?

Deinonychus was the prototype for the "raptors" in the movie "Jurassic Park."

WERE ALL "RAPTORS" ACTUALLY RAPTORS?

Some, but not all, dinosaurs with "raptor" in their name belong to the dromaeosaurid family of feathered dinosaurs. Their titles can be deceptive, though. Many dromaeosaurs don't have "raptor" in their name, such as Deinonychus, Hesperonychus (hess-per-ON-ee-kus), and Saurornitholestes (sore-OR-nith-oh-less-teez). Others, such as Oviraptor and Eoraptor, aren't dromaeosaurs (raptors) at all. True dromaeosaurs include Microraptor, Bambiraptor, Dakotaraptor, Utahraptor, and the famous Velociraptor.

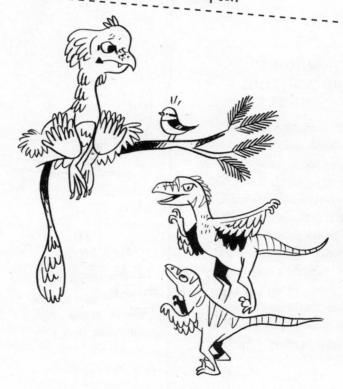

HOW BIG WAS UTAHRAPTOR?

Utahraptor (YOO-tah-rap-tor) was a claw-slashing dromaeosaur closely related to Deinonychus. Although the two looked similar, Utahraptor would have dwarfed Deinonychus. Utahraptor was the largest-ever raptor, and everything about this monster was on a grander scale: its brain, body, claws, and teeth. Utahraptor was around the size of a modern polar bear, with excellent eyesight and sense of smell.

DID UTAHRAPTOR HUNT ALONGSIDE DEINONYCHUS?

Utahraptor was a pack hunter that terrorized the same North American plains as Deinonychus. However, the two cousins were never destined to meet: Utahraptor had been dead for millions of years by the time Deinonychus appeared.

DID ALLOSAURUS AMBUSH ITS PREY?

Hundreds of Allosaurus fossils have been discovered in recent times, so we know a lot about this huge Late Jurassic killer. Allosaurus was the biggest predator of its time and certainly capable of hunting large prey. However, to obtain an advantage, Allosaurus would have lain in wait and then pounced on passing creatures.

DID YOU KNOW?

Allosaurus grew to 12 m (39 ft) long and up to 2,000 kg (4,400 lb) in weight.

HOW DID ALLOSAURUS FEED?

Allosaurus had a larger skull in proportion to its body than many of the other big meat-eaters. It is surprising, then, that Allosaurus had a relatively weak bite. Modern lions, alligators, and leopards all have more powerful jaws than Allosaurus did. For this reason, Allosaurus opened its jaws wide and slammed its head down like a hatchet, forcing its teeth into the flesh. This would have caused massive blood loss and a reasonably fast death.

DID ALLOSAURUS HUNT LARGE PREY?

Allosaurus bite marks found in the fossilized remains of Stegosaurus and some sauropods indicate that it brought down large prey. It may have hunted in packs to do so, as did its allosaur cousins, Sinraptor (SINE-rap-tor) and Yangchuanosaurus (yang-choo-AHN-oh-sore-us).

DID YOU KNOW?

Yangchuanosaurus grew to 10 m (32 ft) tall and up to 3,350 kg (7,390 lb) in weight.

DID VELOCIRAPTOR HUNT IN PACKS?

Velociraptor (vel-OSS-ee-rap-tor), or "swift thief," was a fast, ferocious raptor made famous through its many appearances in dinosaur movies. However, unlike its green, car-sized screen counterparts, Velociraptor was actually the size of a dog and covered in feathers. The films did get one thing right: Velociraptor was a pack hunter.

DID YOU KNOW?

Velociraptor grew up to 2 m (6 ft) long and 15 kg (33 lb) in weight.

WHY DID VELOCIRAPTOR HAVE FEATHERS?

Often dinosaurs had feathers to attract or alarm other dinosaurs, but it is thought that Velociraptor used them for insulation. Feathers would have kept Velociraptor warm as it went about its active, hunting lifestyle.

DID YOU KNOW?

All Velociraptor remains have been found in Asia, in Mongolia and China.

DID VELOCIRAPTOR HAVE A BIG BITE?

Like all of the dromaeosaurs, Velociraptor had claws on its hands and feet and one large, killing claw on its toe. However, unlike some of its raptor cousins, Velociraptor also had a mouth full of 80 sharp, curved teeth. Velociraptor's teeth gave a formidable advantage over its prey, especially when it was hunting in a pack.

DID DASPLETOSAURUSES FIGHT ONE ANOTHER?

When the remains of a Daspletosaurus (das-PLEE-toh-sore-us) was discovered, it was obvious that the dinosaur was an ancestor to T. rex. Daspletosaurus resembled T. rex in almost every way, except it was smaller, heavier, and had longer teeth. The bones also had bite marks made by another Daspletosaurus. This monster had been fighting its own kind.

DID YOU KNOW?

Daspletosaurus grew up to 9 m (30 ft) long and weighed up to 3,700 kg (8,200 lb).

HOW DID DASPLETOSAURUS HUNT?

Like a lion in a pride, Daspletosaurus was a pack hunter that would cooperate with other Daspletosauruses to bring down prey. However, Daspletosaurus was also an opportunist, and it is unlikely that these group kills were well organized. Instead, several Daspletosauruses would have grabbed their chance to join together and attack an isolated plant-eater.

WHY DID DASPLETOSAURUSES FIGHT EACH OTHER?

After a kill was made, it would have been every dinosaur for itself, with the strongest taking all. This explains the Daspletosaurus teeth marks found on the bones of other Daspletosauruses; the killers had been scrapping over pieces of meat.

DID ANY MEAT-EATING DINOSAURS ALSO EAT PLANTS?

Ornithomimus (or-nith-oh-MEE-mus) was a theropod that was unlike any other predatory dinosaur. Most theropods were either hunters that preyed on mammals and other little dinosaurs or large monsters that preyed on the large plant-eaters. But Ornithomimus was neither of these: It was a meat-eater that also ate plants.

DID YOU KNOW?

Ornithomimus grew up to 4 m (13 ft) long and weighed up to 150 kg (330 lb).

HOW DO WE KNOW ORNITHOMIMUS ATE PLANTS?

We know that Ornithomimus ate plants as well as meat because it had a long beak instead of a mouth. This scissorlike beak would have been used to pick up insects and small reptiles, but also to strip and slice through leaves and other plant material.

WAS ORNITHOMIMUS A BIRD?

"Ornithomimus" means "bird mimic," and its feathers and size made it look a lot like a modern ostrich. But Ornithomimus was not a bird: It was a theropod that belonged to the ornithomimid group of dinosaurs. The ornithomimids all had feathers, slender arms and claws, long legs, and could achieve fast running speeds.

DID YOU KNOW?

It is thought that Ornithomimus could reach speeds of 64 km/h (40 mph), making it the fastest dinosaur along with Compsognathus (komp-sog-NATH-us).

DID DINOSAURS EAT FISH?

In 1983, an amateur fossil hunter made a startling discovery in Surrey, England. He unearthed a massive fossil of a 25 cm (10 in) thumb claw. But there was more to come: Beneath the claw was the skeleton of an unknown dinosaur that ate both fish and meat. It was named Baryonyx (bah-ree-ON-iks).

DID YOU KNOW?

Baryonyx grew to 10 m (32 ft) long, 2.5 m (8 ft) high, and up to 5,400 kg (11,900 lb) in weight.

HOW DID WE KNOW BARYONYX ATE BOTH MEAT AND FISH?

Fossils have revealed both fish scales and the remains of an Iguanodon in Baryonyx's stomach. As the largest meat-eating dinosaur discovered in Europe, it seems that Baryonyx could choose what it ate, mixing its diet between land- and water-dwelling prey.

DID YOU KNOW?

Baryonyx belonged to a group of dinosaurs called spinosaurids, which often had large claw thumbs and sails or spikes running down their backs.

HOW DID BARYONYX CATCH FISH?

Baryonyx probably stalked fish from the water's edge or stood in shallow rivers to catch them. Its long, curved claws would have been perfect for holding onto slippery fish. It also poked its snout into the water and grabbed passing fish with its long crocodile-like jaws.

WERE THERE ANY TINY DINOSAUR KILLERS?

Around 75 million years ago, giant meat-eaters like Daspletosaurus and Gorgosaurus prowled the plains, while small, speedy predators like Troodon and Struthiomimus stalked their prey in the forests. Alongside them, however, was an even smaller hunter: Hesperonychus was a killer dinosaur the size of a house cat.

DID YOU KNOW?

Hesperonychus walked on two legs, had razor-sharp hand claws, and a sickle-shaped claw on its toe.

WHO WAS HESPERONYCHUS?

Hesperonychus was a Late Cretaceous killer believed to be the smallest predatory dinosaur in North America. Weighing up to 2 kg (4 lb), reaching 50 cm (1.5 ft) high, and armed with a mouthful of bladelike teeth, Hesperonychus looked like a miniature version of its cousin Velociraptor. But unlike Velociraptor, Hesperonychus probably lived in the trees.

WAS HESPERONYCHUS ABLE TO FLY?

Hesperonychus was covered with feathers, but it could not fly like a bird. Instead, it glided on its wings between the branches of trees as it looked for food. Hesperonychus was small enough to go unnoticed by many large dinosaurs but would have made a good meal for others, so it kept off the forest floor. Hesperonychus's own diet included lizards, insects, and eggs.

DID ALL DINOSAURS FIGHT TO SURVIVE?

The Mesozoic world was one of predators and prey, and every dinosaur had to be ready to fight for its life. Size became a big factor in this battle for survival. As the dinosaur age progressed, sauropods grew to huge proportions.

In response, the theropods also grew bigger, until the two types of dinosaur became locked in an evolutionary size war. Wherever in the world there was a large plant-eater, there was a large meat-eater living alongside it.

DINOSAUR ATTACK

HOW DID PLANT-EATERS PROTECT THEMSELVES?

Size was a plant-eater's best defense against an attacking meat-eater. A massive sauropod like Argentinosaurus was too big to be threatened by a single predator. Other, smaller plant-eaters developed their own individual ways of protecting themselves. These included spikes, horns, and thick plates in their skin.

HOW DID GASTONIA USE ITS SPIKES?

Gastonia (gas-TOH-nee-ah) was a heavily-protected ankylosaur. It grew to 4.6 m (15 ft) in length and weighed up to 3,360 kg (7,400 lb). The spikes along its back stopped enemies such as Utahraptor from leaping up and biting its neck. Gastonia was also able to fight back with its deadly spike-covered tail.

HOW DID CHASMOSAURUS USE ITS FRILL?

Chasmosaurus was a ceratopsian dinosaur and one of the most common to roam the plains of North America. It had a large head frill, but since it was made from thin bone and skin, it would have offered little protection. However, by flushing blood into the skin stretched across the frill, Chasmosaurus may have been able to warn off potential attackers.

DID STEGOSAURUS USE ITS TAIL TO FIGHT?

With the row of plates down its back and the spikes at the end of its tail, Stegosaurus is easy to recognize. The tail is called a thagomizer, and it was an essential weapon against the top predator of the period and Stegosaurus's archenemy: Allosaurus.

DID YOU KNOW?

Stegosaurus grew up to 9 m (30 ft) long, 2.5 m (8 ft) tall, and 3,175 kg (7,000 lb) in weight.

WOULD STEGOSAURUS'S BACK PLATES HAVE PROTECTED IT?

Stegosaurus's back plates were made from bone and skin and used to defend and display. By flushing blood into the skin around the plates, Stegosaurus would have sent a warning for Allosaurus to stay away. The bone in the plates would also have offered some protection, along with a row of tough bone plates along Stegosaurus's neck.

However, these didn't always work, as Allosaurus bite marks to a Stegosaurus neck bone show. Stegosaurus would have put up a good fight though: A hole on an Allosaurus vertebra matches a Stegosaurus thagomizer spike exactly. These two opponents were evenly matched.

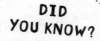

DID YOU KNOW?

Stegosaurus lived during the Late Jurassic period and fossils have been found on several continents.

DID DINOSAURS FIGHT WITH THEIR HEADS?

For many plant-eating dinosaurs, their primary weapon was located on their head. These weapons included spikes and horns on the nose, face, and frill, such as those of the ceratopsian Styracosaurus. Another plant-eater called Pachycephalosaurus (pack-ee-KEF-ah-loh-sore-us) may have used its hard, bony head to butt against attackers.

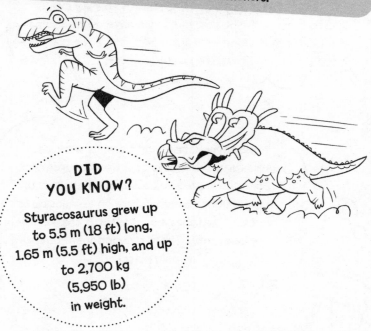

DID YOU KNOW?

Styracosaurus grew up to 5.5 m (18 ft) long, 1.65 m (5.5 ft) high, and up to 2,700 kg (5,950 lb) in weight.

HOW MANY HORNS DID STYRACOSAURUS HAVE?

Styracosaurus had up to nine head horns—more than any other ceratopsian! Small horns on its cheeks ran up to meet longer horns on Styracosaurus's frill. But Styracosaurus's nose horn was the longest of all, and at 30 cm (2 ft) long, it would have been deadly against predators such as Daspletosaurus.

WAS PACHYCEPHALOSAURUS A HEAD-BUTTER?

One of the strangest dinosaurs ever discovered, Pachycephalosaurus had a thick head dome made from 25cm (10 in) of solid bone. This prompted the theory that Pachycephalosaurus used its dome to headbutt enemies and rival Pachycephalosauruses. A discovery in 2012 supported this theory. A Pachycephalosaurus skull was unearthed that showed damage that had probably resulted from headbutting.

In 1971, the skeleton of a Velociraptor was found wrapped around the skeleton of a Protoceratops (proh-toh-SERRA-tops), preserved in a life-and-death struggle. As Protoceratops bit down into Velociraptor's arm and Velociraptor slashed at Protoceratops's throat, a sandstorm swept in and buried them both alive. Their fight remained frozen in time forever.

DID YOU KNOW?

Protoceratops grew up to 1.8 m (5.9 ft) long, 67 cm (25 in) high, and weighed up to 400 kg (880 lb).

WERE ANY OTHER ATTACKING DINOSAURS FROZEN IN TIME?

Incredibly, another fossilized Velociraptor and Protoceratops fight was discovered in 2008. This time, the Velociraptor skeleton is feeding on the Protoceratops skeleton. Experts think that in this instance, Velociraptor was scavenging from the already dead Protoceratops corpse, rather than attacking it. This is because of the deep bite marks Velociraptor had left on the Protoceratops skeleton. It had even broken a couple of its teeth on the bones. This indicated that Velociraptor was trying to scrape off the last pieces of meat left on the bone, which meant that the predator was scavenging from a dead animal.

DID YOU KNOW?

About the size of a sheep, Protoceratops was a common Asian dinosaur and prey for Velociraptor.

DID MEAT-EATING DINOSAURS OFTEN FIGHT?

As a rule, different species of large, predatory dinosaurs tried to avoid each other. Each dominated its own patch, and unless food became scarce, it was not worth waging a territorial war. However, occasionally, such battles did take place. We know about one between Spinosaurus (SPY-noh-sore-us) and Carcharodontosaurus, two of the largest predators to walk the Earth.

DID YOU KNOW?

Carcharodontosaurus grew to 15 m long, (49 ft), 2.75 m (9 ft) high, and 7,500 kg (16,500 lb) in weight.

WHO WAS CARCHARODONTOSAURUS?

During the Late Cretaceous period, Carcharodontosaurus was the largest land hunter in North Africa. Its head was larger than T. rex's, and it contained a mouthful of long, bladelike teeth like a shark's. Carcharodontosaurus needed to eat 60 kg (130 lb) of meat every day to survive, and each one defended a piece of territory around 500 sq km (200 sq miles).

DID YOU KNOW?

Carcharodontosaurus, or "shark-toothed lizard," was named after the Great White Shark (Carcharodon) because of the resemblance between their serrated teeth.

DID ARGENTINOSAURUS HAVE A PREDATOR?

Argentinosaurus was the largest land animal that ever lived, and it was thought unlikely that there was a predator big enough to hunt it. But in 2006, a new discovery made experts think again. A new, 13 m (43 ft) long killer had been found, and it was capable of hunting a giant like Argentinosaurus.

DID YOU KNOW?

Mapusaurus grew to 13 m long (42 ft) and weighed up to 2,995 kg (6,600 lb).

WHO WAS MAPUSAURUS?

Mapusaurus (MAH-puh-sore-us) was the predator that preyed on Argentinosaurus. However, it was too small to do this alone. Instead, several Mapusauruses worked as a group to attack the great sauropod. One such group was discovered in a South American fossil bed in 2006. The skeletons of several Mapusauruses of different ages proved the theory that the killer was a pack hunter.

HOW DID MAPUSAURUS HUNT?

Experts think that even a Mapusaurus pack would not have been able to bring down an adult Argentinosaurus. Instead, they think Mapusaurus took nonlethal bites out of Argentinosaurus's body but left the dinosaur standing. Mapusaurus's bladelike teeth were perfectly designed to slice off pieces of flesh in this way. By treating Argentinosaurus's body like a table to take a snack from, Mapusaurus could come back and snack again in the future.

DID YOU KNOW?

Mapusaurus was closely related to Giganotosaurus, which also roamed the plains of South America.

DID TRICERATOPS EVER FIGHT T. REX?

Triceratops and T. rex were the two mightiest dinosaurs to prowl the plains and forests of Late Cretaceous North America. The image of T. rex, its jaws bristling with bone-crunching teeth, battling the tank-shaped Triceratops, with its face full of horns, is spectacular and terrifying. But there is very little evidence of a T. rex and Triceratops battle.

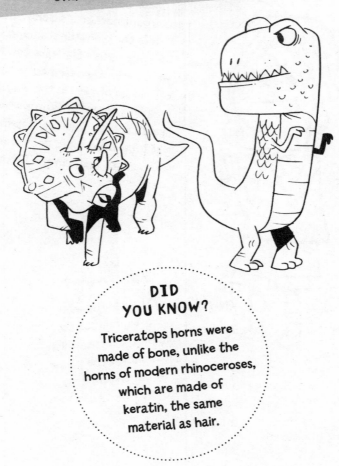

DID YOU KNOW?

Triceratops horns were made of bone, unlike the horns of modern rhinoceroses, which are made of keratin, the same material as hair.

DID T. REX EAT TRICERATOPS?

Fossils have shown T. rex's bite marks on Triceratops bones, but these are thought to have occurred after death. In other words, T. rex probably scavenged from a Triceratops carcass after it was already dead. More gruesomely, the injuries show that T. rex removed Triceratops's head to get at the nutrient-rich flesh in its neck.

DID YOU KNOW?

Other fossils show that T. rex may have fed on young Triceratops, which would have stood no chance against the giant killer.

WERE DINOSAURS CANNIBALS?

During the Late Cretaceous period, two types of killer dinosaurs dominated the Earth. The northern hemisphere was ruled by the tyrannosaurs and the southern hemisphere, by the abelisaurs. Abelisaurs were just as dangerous and deadly as their northern counterparts and also had a disturbing habit: cannibalism.

DID YOU KNOW?

Majungasaurus was an abelisaur that grew to 9 m (30 ft) long, 3.75 m (12 ft) high, and weighed up to 2,100 kg (4,630) lb.

WHO WAS MAJUNGASAURUS?

Majungasaurus (mah-JOONG-gah-sore-us) was a common abelisaur that left many fossils behind. The bones of these fossils have revealed a series of deep bite marks made by other Majungasauruses. These marks show that the dinosaurs not only fought each other, but that they also ate the flesh off each other's bones. It is the first direct evidence of cannibalism in dinosaurs.

HOW DID MAJUNGASAURUS KILL?

Abelisaurs had a much shorter skull than the tyrannosaurs and a different way of killing their prey. Instead of tearing chunks off a victim until it was dead, Majungasaurus would have clamped its jaws full of sharp teeth down tight on its prey's neck. This bite-and-hold technique was similar to that used by modern lions and was brutally effective.

DID YOU KNOW?

When it wasn't attacking its own kind, Majungasaurus fed on long-necked sauropods.

WERE ANY DINOSAURS POISONOUS?

The discovery of Sinornithosaurus (sine-OR-nith-oh-sore-us) was a world-changing moment in the study of dinosaurs. The feathers covering this so-called "fuzzy raptor" were almost identical to that of modern birds. Sinornithosaurus was a true ancestor to the birds. But there was more: It also had specially shaped teeth that could inject poison into its prey.

DID YOU KNOW?

Sinornithosaurus grew up to 2 m (6.5 ft) long and was up to 4.5 kg (10 lb) in weight.

WHAT WERE SINORNITHOSAURUS'S TEETH LIKE?

Sinornithosaurus had long, fang-like teeth with a groove running down the surface. This type of tooth is usually only seen in venomous animals, such as snakes. Experts think a venom gland in the jaw fed poison into the teeth. When Sinornithosaurus bit into its victim with its fangs, the poison would then have stunned or killed its prey.

DID YOU KNOW?

Sinornithosaurus lived in the forests of China during the Early Cretaceous period.

COULD SINORNITHOSAURUS FLY?

Although its feathers were similar to that of modern birds, it could not fly in the same way. Rather than flapping its wings to lift itself into the air, Sinornithosaurus would have used them to glide between tree branches or down to the ground to attack its prey.

RECORD-BREAKING DINOSAURS

WHY WERE DINOSAURS RECORD-BREAKERS?

By their very nature, dinosaurs were record-breakers. They dominated the globe for tens of millions of years and in that time were among the largest, longest, and most lethal creatures the world has ever known. But dinosaurs weren't only famous for their size and strength: Some were smart, others stupid, and some were the speediest creatures around.

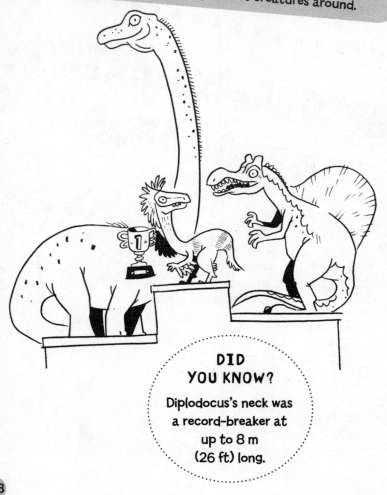

DID YOU KNOW?

Diplodocus's neck was a record-breaker at up to 8 m (26 ft) long.

WHICH DINOSAUR HAD THE LONGEST TAIL?

Diplodocus wasn't the longest sauropod ever, but it probably had the longest tail. Its tail measured up to 13 m (45 ft) long, which is longer than a bus. Diplodocus's tail was so long that it contained over 80 separate bones, whereas most sauropods only had 40.

COULD DIPLODOCUS WHIP ITS TAIL?

At the end of Diplodocus's tail were small, tube-shaped vertebrae that would have made a dangerous whip. Many sauropods used their tail as a whip to fend off predators, and it is likely that Diplodocus did the same. Diplodocus would have also used its tail to balance itself when it reared up on its hind feet.

DID YOU KNOW?

Despite its long neck, Diplodocus had a very small head at only around 60 cm (2 ft) long.

WHICH DINOSAUR WAS THE BIGGEST?

The biggest dinosaur was also the largest creature ever to walk on land: Argentinosaurus. Argentinosaurus lived during the Early Cretaceous period in South America. It was half the length of a 747 passenger plane, weighed the same as 1,000 grown men, and was tall enough to have peered through the windows of a building four floors high.

DID ARGENTINOSAURUS LAY BIG EGGS?

Argentinosaurus eggs were about the size of footballs. More impressive is the number of eggs it laid. An enormous fossil bed in Argentina has revealed tens of thousands of Argentinosaurus eggs. It is thought that the site was used as a nesting site for the sauropod over millions of years, with each one laying hundreds of eggs annually.

DID ARGENTINOSAURUS HAVE ANY BIG RIVALS?

Another sauropod dinosaur found in Argentina in 2014 has the statistics to rival Argentinosaurus. This titanosaur dinosaur grew up to 37 m (122 ft) long, weighed 63,502 kg (140,000 lb), and was 6 m (20 ft) tall. Although this meant that the monster was as long as three buses and heavier than 10 African elephants, it still did not match up to Argentinosaurus.

WHICH WAS THE BIGGEST DINOSAUR PREDATOR?

The largest land carnivore ever seen on Earth was Spinosaurus. Spinosaurus roamed the swamps of North Africa during the Cretaceous Period. It was a colossal killer with a list of massive measurements. It was longer than two buses, taller than a giraffe, and weighed more than 30 lions. It also had a skull measuring 2 m (6.5 ft). That's the longest of any theropod dinosaur.

DID YOU KNOW?

Spinosaurus grew up to 18 m (60 ft) long, 3 m (10 ft) high, and weighed up to 5,500 kg (12,000 lb).

COULD SPINOSAURUS SWIM?

Spinosaurus couldn't swim, but it was an expert fisherman. High-placed nostrils and small sensor holes on the end of its nose allowed Spinosaurus to stick its snout deep into the water to detect prey. It could then grab fish without even seeing them in its specially curved claws and jaws full of cone-shaped teeth.

WHY DID SPINOSAURUS HAVE A SAIL?

A row of spines sticking up from Spinosaurus's back formed a sail that was almost 2 m (6.5 ft) high. Covered with skin, this sail may have acted as a way of collecting heat from the sun and releasing heat during hot temperatures. It could also have been used to signal to a mate.

WHICH DINOSAUR WAS **THE SMARTEST?**

The smartest dinosaur is thought to be Troodon. That is because this meat-eater had the biggest brain in relation to its body size of any dinosaur. Even so, it was no Einstein; it is thought that Troodon had a similar level of intelligence to modern-day birds.

$$Gui=89I\ G(Tw+tP)$$

DID YOU KNOW?

Troodon's brain was about the size of a modern emu's. Emus also have large eyes for their size, giving them good eyesight.

COULD TROODON HUNT AT NIGHT?

Troodon had extremely big eyes, which allowed it to see more in low-light conditions. The Troodons of Alaska used this well-adapted eyesight to hunt at night, something that was not possible for most other predators. Troodons often targeted young Edmontosauruses under the cover of night. The Alaskan Troodons were so successful in this that they grew to twice the size of Troodons anywhere else in the world.

HOW BIG WAS TROODON?

Troodon was about the size of a large dog. It was also fast. Troodon had long, thin legs and a large toe claw, which it could retract like a cat's when it was running. It was also a pack hunter and made good use of its speed and high intelligence to outsmart its prey.

WHICH DINOSAURS WERE THE FASTEST?

The small- to medium-sized theropods were the fastest runners of the dinosaur world. However, calculating any dinosaur's running speed can be a tricky task. To do this, the dinosaur's footprints left in trackways have to be measured against its fossilized leg bones. This gives a speed estimate. The graph below shows how some of the dinosaur runners compare with modern-day animals.

T. rex: 29 km/h (18 mph)

Allosaurus: 34 km/h (21 mph)

DID YOU KNOW?

The fastest speed for a human to run a 100 m race is 9.58 seconds, which equals an average of 37.5 km/h (23 mph). A human could outrun a T. rex!

DID YOU KNOW?

Ornithomimus would have been able to run a 100 m race in 5.59 seconds. That's nearly twice as fast as Olympic sprinter Usain Bolt.

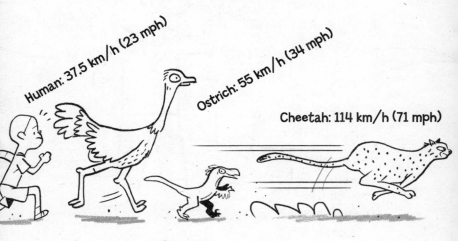

Human: 37.5 km/h (23 mph)

Ostrich: 55 km/h (34 mph)

Cheetah: 114 km/h (71 mph)

Ornithomimus: 64 km/h (40 mph)

WHICH DINOSAUR HAD THE SMALLEST BRAIN?

With its distinctive back plates and spiked tail, Stegosaurus is one of the most famous plant-eating dinosaurs. It was also one of the stupidest. Although it weighed more than a rhinoceros, Stegosaurus had the brain the size of a walnut. This is especially surprising because Stegosaurus's head was the same size as the head of a horse.

DID YOU KNOW?

The dromaeosaur dinosaurs, such as Troodon, had the biggest brains for their body size.

DID THE MEAT-EATERS HAVE SMALL BRAINS?

Dinosaur predators needed to be smarter than the plant-eaters that they preyed upon. There was a high failure rate among hunting meat-eaters, so they had to try to outsmart their quarry. As such, a meat-eater's brain was highly developed in the regions of smell and sight. However, the large theropods still had remarkably small brains. Giganotosaurus, one of the biggest predators, had a brain the size of a banana.

DID YOU KNOW?

Although Stegosaurus had one of the smallest brains, it is thought that the large sauropods could have been even less intelligent.

WHICH DINOSAUR WAS THE WEIRDEST?

There were lots of odd dinosaurs, from the headbutting Pachycephalosaurus' to the ill-equipped Iguanodon, which had only a thumb spike for protection. But perhaps the strangest of all was Therizinosaurus (THER-ih-zine-oh-sore-us). Therizinosaurus was a large theropod with a twist: It had given up eating meat to become a vegetarian.

WHY DID THERIZINOSAURUS GIVE UP MEAT?

Experts think that Therizinosaurus was formerly a meat-eater: It belonged to the same theropod family as T. rex and was armed with claws that appeared perfect for slashing flesh. However, it seems that there was so much competition for meat among the other theropods of the time that Therizinosaurus became a plant-eater instead.

DID THERIZINOSAURUS HAVE THE LARGEST CLAWS?

Therizinosaurus's sickle-shaped claws measured up to 1 m (3.3 ft) long (which is as long as a baseball bat) and are the largest claws of any creature that walked the Earth. When Therizinosaurus was first discovered, it baffled paleontologists. At first, it was believed to be a large turtle, as its claws were thought to be giant flippers. However, Therizinosaurus did not have sharp teeth like other theropods. Instead, it had peg-shaped teeth that were perfect for stripping leaves from branches.

DID YOU KNOW?

Therizinosaurus grew to 10 m (33 ft) in length and 5,000 kg (11,000 lb) in weight.

WHICH WERE THE SMALLEST DINOSAURS?

A large number of small dinosaurs came and went during the Mesozoic Era. Every time scientists think they have discovered the smallest-ever dinosaur, another even tinier one is found to take its place.

MICRORAPTOR

This was a crow-sized killer around 80 cm long (31 in) long and 2 kg (4.4 lb) in weight. It lived in China during the Early Cretaceous period.

ANCHIORNIS (ANG-KEE-OR-NIS)

This kitten-sized, feathered dinosaur grew up to 34 cm (13 in) long. It lived in China during the Jurassic Period and, at only 110 g (3.9 oz), is the lightest dinosaur ever discovered.

COMPSOGNATHUS

A chicken-sized theropod, this dinosaur was around 65 cm (26 in) long and 3.6 kg (8 lb) in weight. It stalked its prey in Europe during the Late Jurassic period.

HESPERONYCHUS

This was a pigeon-sized Late Cretaceous predator from North America that grew up to 50 cm (1.5 ft) long and 2 kg (4 lb).

DID YOU KNOW?

The first vertebrates to develop true flight were the pterosaurs, but they later shared the skies with Microraptor and early birds.

WHICH DINOSAUR HAD THE BIGGEST HEAD?

The dinosaurs with the largest heads were the horned and frilled herbivores known as the ceratopsians. The heads of these giants were so big that they sometimes made up 40 % of their overall body length. The award for biggest-ever head goes jointly to two ceratopsian cousins: Torosaurus (tor-OH-sore-us) and Pentaceratops (pen-tah-SERRA-tops).

DID YOU KNOW?

It is thought that the frills of both Pentaceratops and Torosaurus were brightly shaded and used for display.

HOW BIG WAS TOROSAURUS'S HEAD?

Torosaurus was closely related to Triceratops and had a similar frill and horns. The length of Torosaurus's head, which includes its frill, was 2.77 m (9.1 ft). That's as long as a small car! Torosaurus's skull is thought to be the longest of any known land animal that has lived on Earth.

HOW BIG WAS PENTACERATOPS'S HEAD?

Pentaceratops was a cousin to Torosaurus that lived slightly earlier in the Late Cretaceous period. There was little difference between the skulls of Pentaceratops and Torosaurus, but Pentaceratops's was slightly smaller. It measured 2.75 m (9 ft) in length.

DID YOU KNOW?

The frills of Pentaceratops and Torosaurus were made from thin bone with two large openings in the middle, so they would not have been used for protection.

WHICH WAS THE BIGGEST FEATHERED DINOSAUR?

The bones of the largest feathered dinosaur were found by accident in 2005. Paleontologists were making a film in China about sauropod bones when they discovered a mysterious bone buried among them. It was the leg bone of Gigantoraptor (gig-ANT-oh-rap-tor): the biggest feathered creature that ever walked the Earth. It was similar in appearance to another strange theropod: Therizinosaurus.

DID YOU KNOW?

Gigantoraptor had a beak for a mouth, and it is thought that it ate plants, insects, and small mammals, but no one is sure.

HOW BIG WAS GIGANTORAPTOR?

At over 2,200 kg (4,850 lb), Gigantoraptor weighed more than 14 ostriches, which is the heaviest feathered creature alive today. Gigantoraptor was also 8 m (26 ft) long, which is 35 times larger than its nearest oviraptor cousin and not much smaller than T. rex. Like other oviraptors, Gigantoraptor was armed with large killing claws on its feet and could easily outrun most theropod predators. Gigantoraptor had wings but flapped them only in display. It also laid some of the biggest dinosaur eggs ever discovered.

WERE THERE OTHER LARGE, FEATHERED DINOSAURS?

Among the other large, feathered dinosaurs was Beipiaosaurus (BAY-pyow-sore-us). Beipiaosaurus was the largest feathered dinosaur when it was discovered in 1999, but at 2.2 m (7.3 ft) in length, it would have been dwarfed by Gigantoraptor.